THE ABCs of Christ's Christmas

Shakera Reid-Stewart

**All rights reserved.
Copyright© 2025**

A IS FOR ANGELS.

B IS FOR BETHLEHEM.

D IS FOR THE **D**ONKEY THAT MARY RODE TO BETHLEHEM.

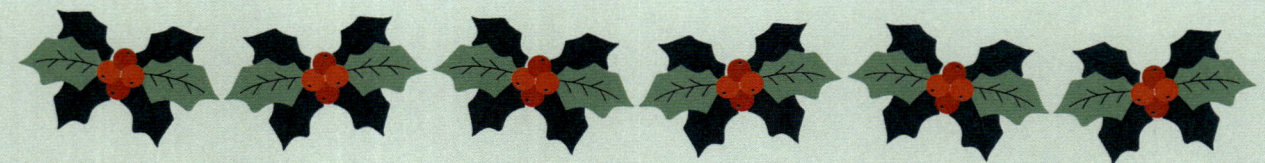

E

IS FOR GOD'S **E**VERLASTING LOVE.

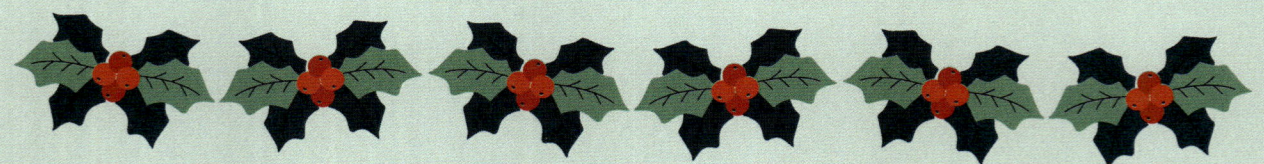

F IS FOR FAITHFULNESS.

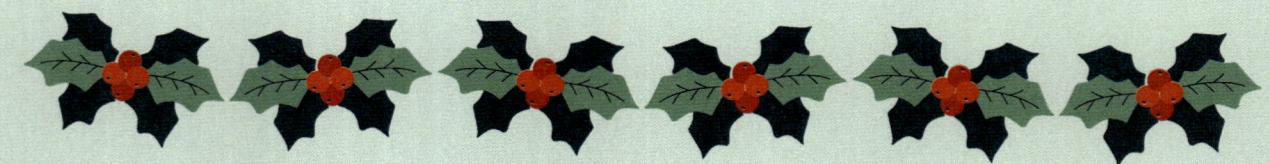

G IS FOR **G**IFTS OF GOLD, FRANKINCENSE, AND MYRRH.

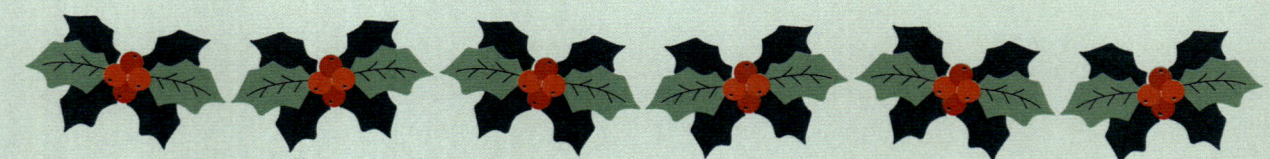

H

IS FOR HOPE FOR THE HOPELESS.

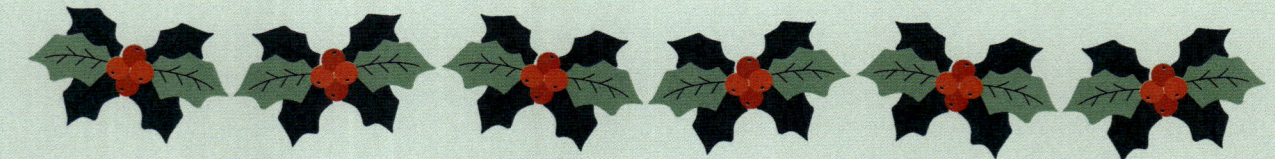

I IS FOR IMMANUEL.

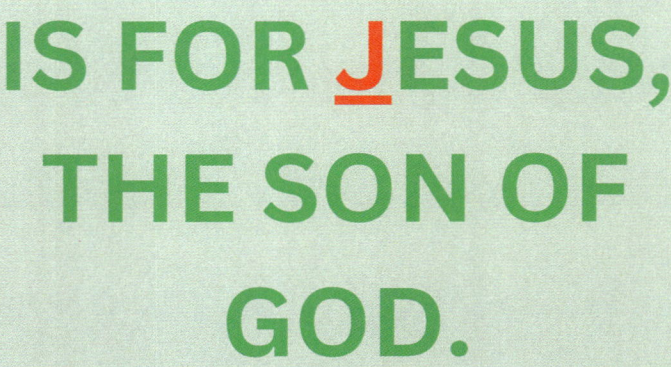

J IS FOR JESUS, THE SON OF GOD.

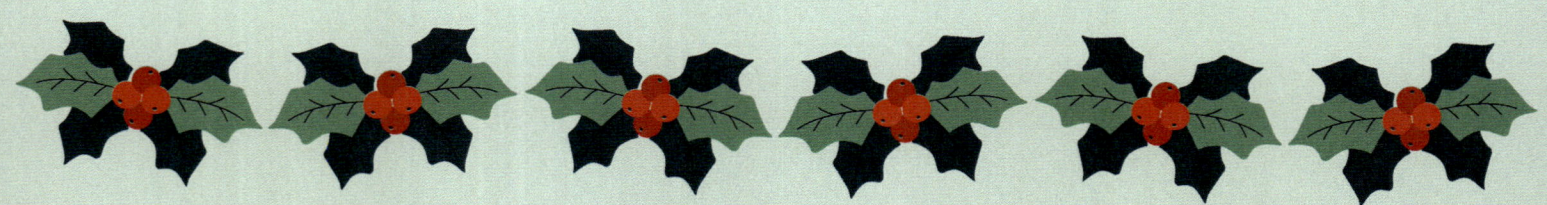

K

IS FOR THE EVIL KING HEROD.

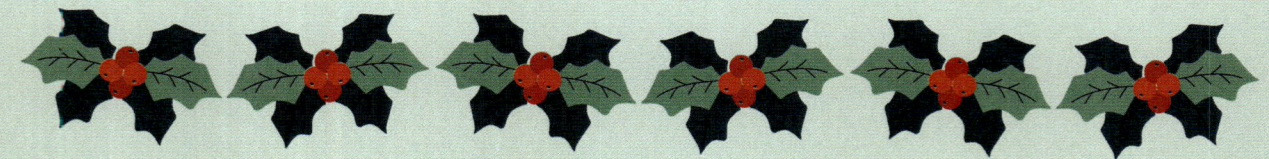

L IS FOR LIGHT OF THE WORLD.

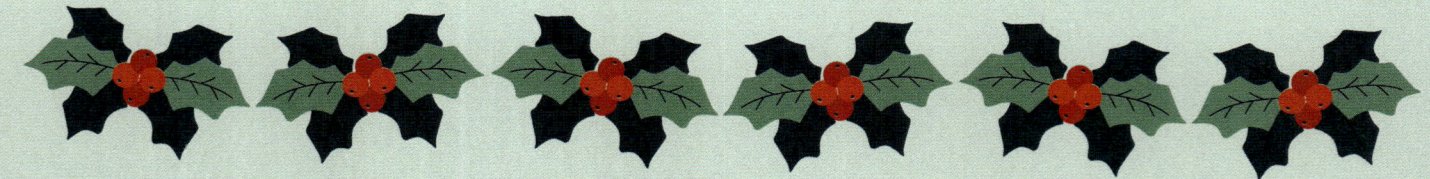

M IS FOR THE **M**ANGER IN THE STABLE WHERE JESUS LAID.

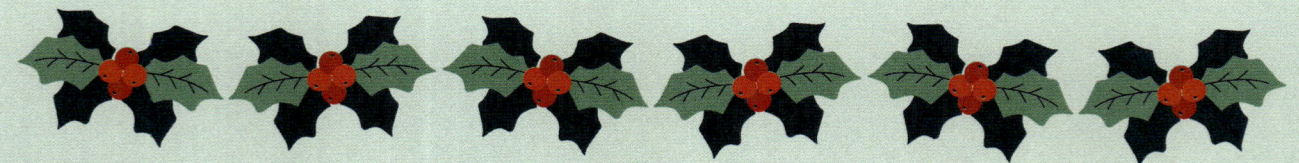

N IS FOR "NO ROOM IN THE INN."

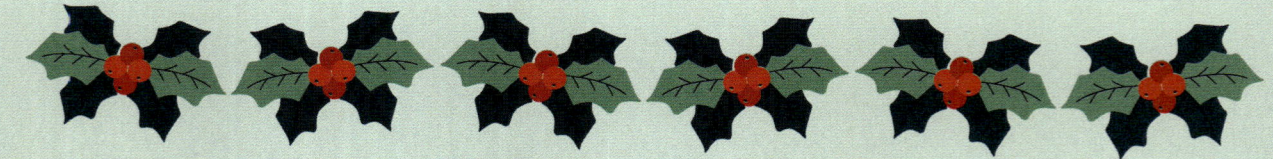

O

IS FOR
O HOLY
NIGHT.

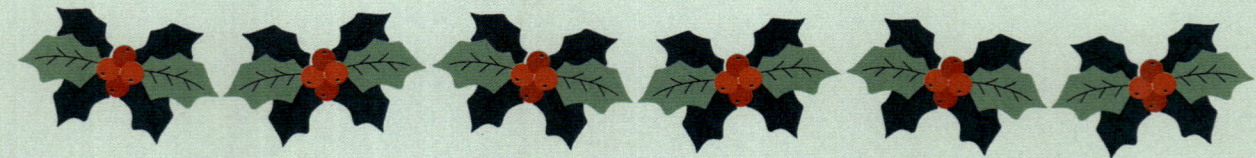

P

IS FOR PEACE ON EARTH.

Q IS FOR THE QUEST TO FIND THE BABY KING.

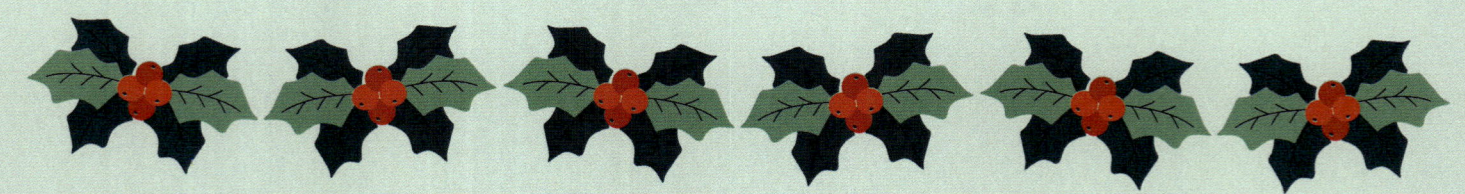

R IS FOR REJOICING.

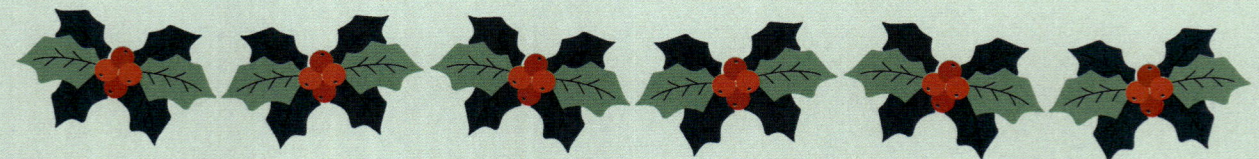

S IS FOR THE SHEPHERDS WATCHING THEIR FLOCK BY NIGHT.

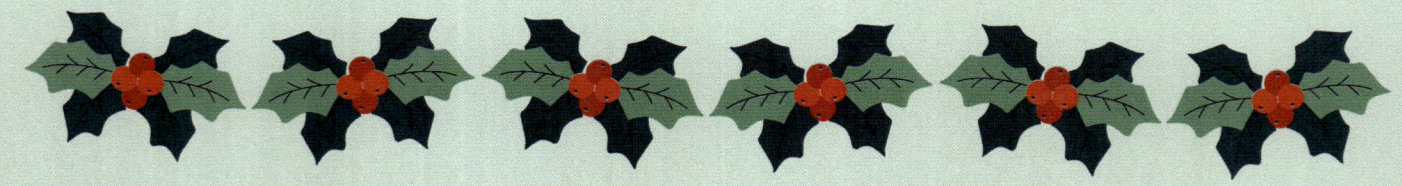

T IS FOR, "TELL IT ON THE MOUNTAIN THAT JESUS CHRIST IS BORN.

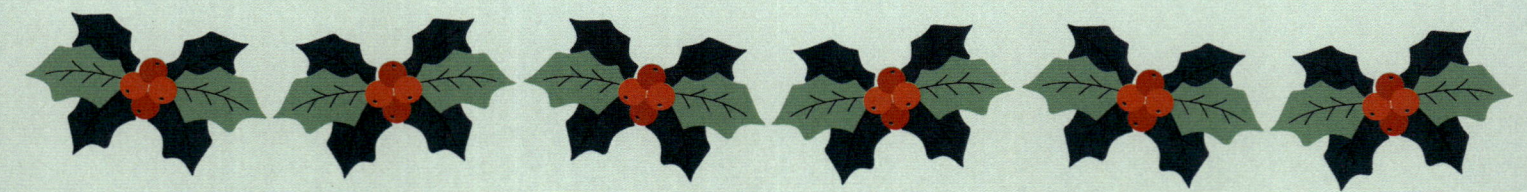

U IS FOR A **U**NIVERSAL GIFT OF SALVATION.

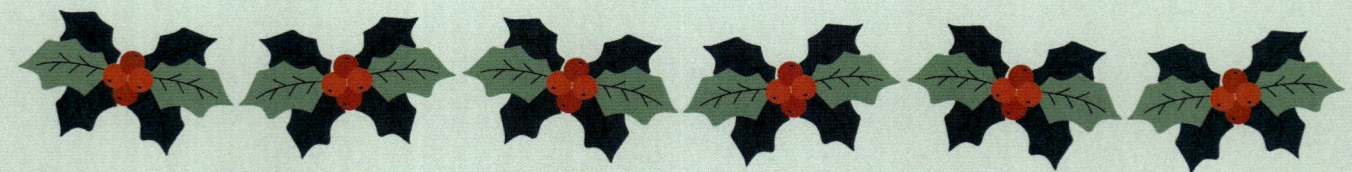

V IS FOR THE VIRGIN MARY, MOTHER OF JESUS.

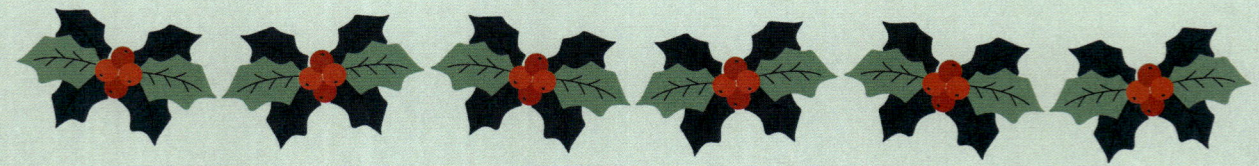

W IS FOR WISE MEN.

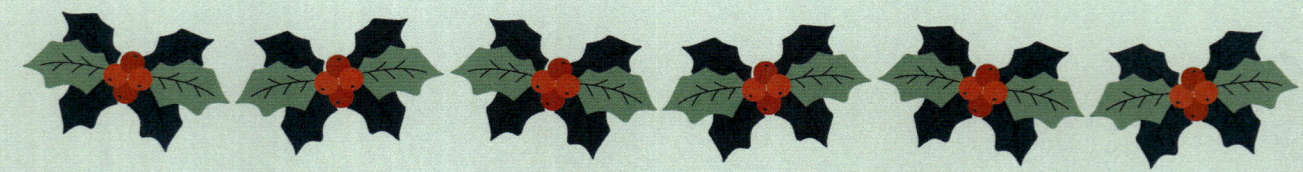

X IS FOR EXCITING NEWS.

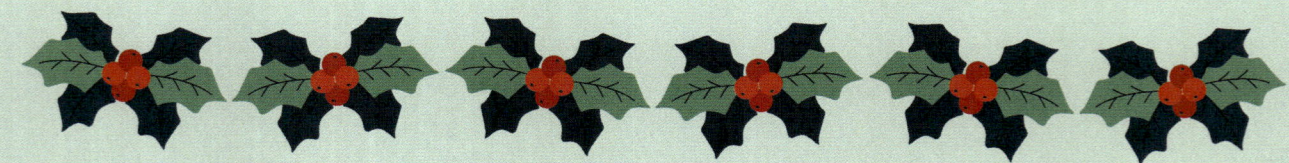

Y

Y IS FOR **Y**OUR CHANCE TO BE FORGIVEN AND TO BE BORN AGAIN

Z IS FOR GOD'S AMAZING GRACE.

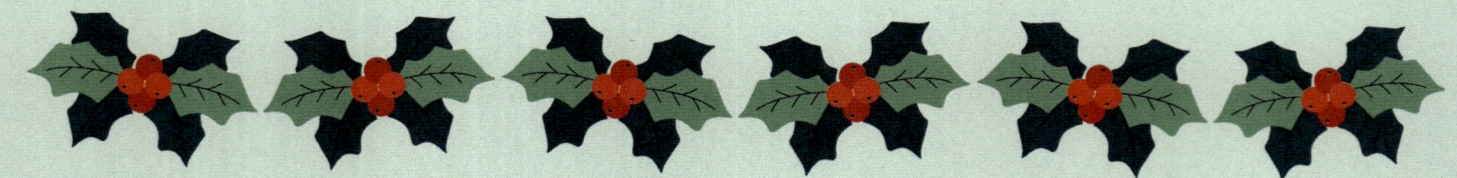

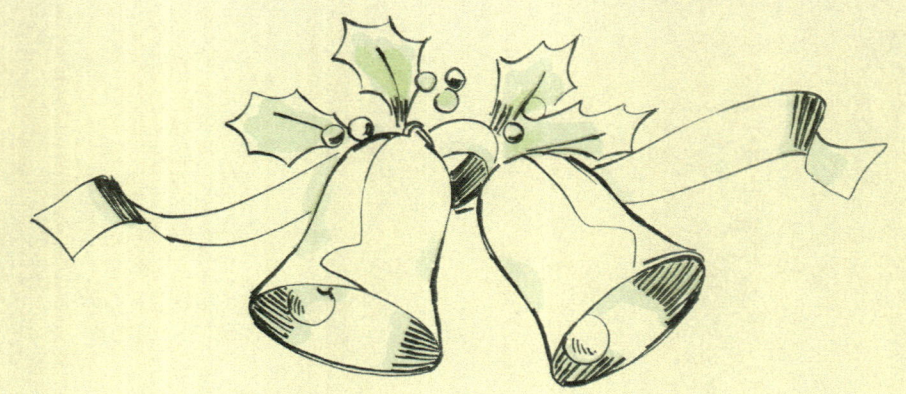

LUKE 2:11, 14 KJV

FOR UNTO YOU IS BORN THIS DAY, IN THE CITY OF DAVID, A SAVIOR WHO IS CHRIST THE LORD.

GLORY TO GOD IN THE HIGHEST, AND ON EARTH PEACE, GOOD WILL TOWARD MEN.

Made in the USA
Coppell, TX
20 January 2026

69541876R00033